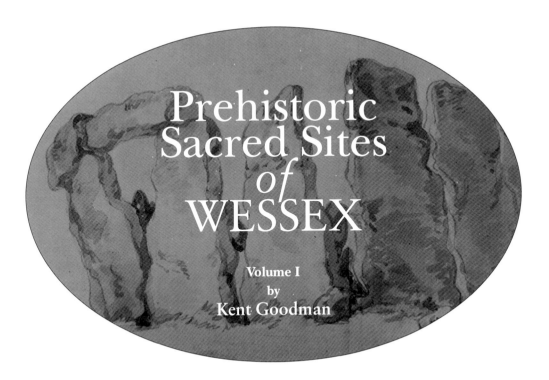

Prehistoric Sacred Sites *of* WESSEX

Volume I

by

Kent Goodman

is placed on a small wooden platform, left for the elements to pick his bones clean. They know that within another month his body will be added to the others in the tomb, as further proof to all neighbouring tribes that this land is guarded by the spirits of their ancestors.

As the evening grows darker, the small band wind their way homeward, torches spluttering. Peering across the sacred landscape, they can see the outline of a large circular ring, its few standing stones a reminder of the proper time for the great seasonal celebrations. The stones are alive, the fields of corn are alive, the river is alive. All around them they can feel the energy – the slow, almost imperceptible heartbeat of the Great Mother Goddess.

Foreword

Below:
This tree grows on the bank of the henge. J.R.R. Tolkien is said to have drawn his inspiration for Lord of the Rings *while sitting under it.*

The ancient kingdom of Wessex is an enchanted land filled with churches and cathedrals. And although there are many fine examples of these places of worship, the sanctity of the area goes back much farther – all the way to the very first hunter/farmers. These Neolithic people built a large number of sacred hills, camps, rings and mounds in which to honour the dead, celebrate the seasons and mark territorial boundaries.

Living in close harmony with their natural environment, these people would have had a very powerful relationship with their gods. Archaeological evidence shows us that Stonehenge and Avebury were in use as sacred sites for as long as Christianity has been known.

The sheer number and variety of prehistoric sacred sites in Wessex makes it necessary to divide the subject into two volumes. In this book, we will examine two of the most important sites in all of Britain – the Stonehenge and Avebury ritual complexes. In a following book, we will look at the different styles of monuments, such as dolmens, standing stones and quoits, that are apparent in south-western Wessex.

We hope this book will give the reader a brief glimpse of life here thousands of years ago, when family was everything and each person was bound completely to the soil beneath his feet and the moon and sun above.

Sacred Landscapes

THE AVEBURY COMPLEX was undoubtedly one of the most important areas in all of Britain, if not Northern Europe, during the Neolithic and Early Bronze Ages. Avebury should be viewed as a complex of ritual constructions that include (in chronological order): the causewayed camp of Windmill Hill; the funerary house called the Sanctuary; the West Kennet Long Barrow; the first stage of Silbury Hill; the West Kennet and Beckhampton Avenues and the henge itself. It should also be noted that ritual landscapes are always connected with water, and the Avebury Complex stands near the confluence of two important rivers, the Winterbourne and the Kennet.

Avebury itself is a henge, a ritual area, roughly circular in shape, surrounded by a deep ditch and bank. Why make it circular? A circle is the perfect natural shape. Then again, some crop circles are apparently formed by vortexes of air that descend to the earth, scribing a circular shape. If a primitive farmer saw this occurring, he might easily think it a direct sign from the gods, and either erect a monument inside the circumference, or attempt to replicate the shape, although it seems an ambitious undertaking! Like all other henges, Avebury is Neolithic, raised between 3710 BC and 2000 BC. This is approximately the same time that the pyramids were being built in Egypt. Thirteen of the great pyramids could fit inside the Avebury circle! Henges are

The Avebury Complex

Henges

Avebury is the largest henge in Britain, so large, in fact, that the village is encompassed by its banks.

associated with ceremonies involving the seasons, and important passages in the lives of people. If we empty our minds of modern images, we can imagine a Neolithic farming community coming together to celebrate the summer harvest and midwinter moonrise, with great orgies of feasting and dancing and displays of fertility.

The sarsens (named after Saracen, meaning heathen), were never artificially formed, as at Stonehenge, but were chosen carefully for their shape from the sarsen fields on the Marlborough Downs. From there the stones, which weighed between 10 and 60 tonnes, were dragged to Avebury, presumably on wooden sledges with rollers. Once on site, they were set up in pits about 3 feet deep, apparently at random with regard to shape, except for the

Sarsens

Avebury is massive, although the henge's sheer scale is hard to appreciate. However, it was second only to Silbury Hill in terms of the amount of labour required to build it. The outer ditch and bank enclose an area of 28 ½ acres, separated by four causeways. The ditch was originally up to 33 feet (10 metres) deep, and 70 feet (23 metres) wide, with the bank towering 55 feet (nearly 17 metres) above the ditch. We have to remember that all of this excavation was done by hand. Deer antler picks and rakes and ox scapula shovels were used to hack out the chalk, which was then shovelled into baskets or leather buckets, finally to be hauled up and piled to form the bank. This chalk rubble would have

made the bank stand out stark and white against the surroundings.

There are actually three stone circles (made of sarsen) in Avebury. The outer circle, which consists of 98 stones, and two smaller inner circles. One is aligned north and includes the Cove, three huge flat stones making a square enclosure with an open side. The other circle is aligned south, and featured the 21 foot tall stone Obelisk, which itself was surrounded by 29 smaller stones set at intervals of 36 feet (the intervals were the same for all the stones at Avebury). Altogether, Avebury used 247 stones for the circles. The whole of Stonehenge could easily fit into either of the smaller circles.

Avebury, 'does as much exceed in greatness the so renowned Stonehenge, as a cathedral doeth a parish church', declared John Aubrey, in the seventeenth century.

This ancient site had become almost completely forgotten by the middle ages, so Aubrey's excitement at its discovery (made whilst he was out fox-hunting on the Marlborough Downs), is understandable.

Nearly one hundred years later William Stukeley visited the area, when the local farmers were doing all they could to destroy the stones, either for building material or just to get them out of the way of the plough. One method was to dig a big pit next to a stone, and topple the sarsen over into it. At least one person, probably a travelling doctor judging from the scissors and iron probe found on him, got his just deserts when a stone he was directing into a pit fell on him, killing him instantly.

flat, square Swindon stone, set at an angle at the north entrance, and the two portal stones at the south. It would probably have taken 500 men nearly a million hours of hard work to complete the ceremonial centre.

Many people assume henges were incredibly complicated observatories, and to be sure, sightlines at all of them show the major sunrises and moonrises at the equinoxes. However, since they were built in a rather haphazard way, that couldn't have been their prime function. They were more likely places for meetings, celebrations and mass gatherings. Great emphasis is placed on fertility rites, in most primitive farming communities; they were almost certainly carried out here. At the opposite end, we know that funerary rites were also held because several of the stones have human remains buried next to them. In the same way, the bank and ditch held remains, but only of skulls, mandibles and long bones. This suggests that certain parts of the body were removed for special ceremonies, whilst the rest were buried in another area – in this case, the Sanctuary. There was only one complete burial at Avebury, that of a female dwarf, surrounded by small sarsens, deer antlers and animal bones, buried at the end of one of the ditches. She was probably a dedicatory sacrifice.

The purpose of henges

Below:
Some scholars have commented on the similarity between the design of the Avebury ritual landscape and Egyptian sun and snake motifs.

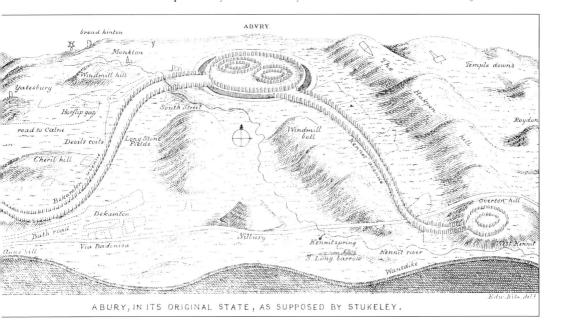

ABURY, IN ITS ORIGINAL STATE, AS SUPPOSED BY STUKELEY.

The Sanctuary

Between 300 and 400 stones were used to erect the West Kennet and Beckhampton Avenues, two long rows of stones, alternating wide (female) and long (male) shapes, that travel over a mile to the Sanctuary on Overton Hill. The Sanctuary is one of the oldest sites in the complex, started just after the completion of Windmill Hill. Originally a round wooden structure, it was used as an area where the recently deceased would be left to the elements until only bones remained (it might possibly have been used for puberty and fertility rites, based on anthropological evidence). No doubt it was accompanied by feasting and celebrations, after which the utensils and food would be buried in pits, first being broken to release their spirit. The original site was used until the structure was rotting away, after which it was rebuilt on a larger and grander scale. It was finally ringed with stone, and connected

These two stones sit in a field outside the henge, and are two of the remaining stones of the Beckhampton Avenue. Known as the Adam and Eve stones, they are said to be the protectors of the sacred site.

to Avebury by Beckhampton Avenue. The West Kennet Avenue travelled over a mile and a half in the other direction. These processionals re-emphasised the Sanctuary's importance once Avebury was built.

It is obvious from the many stone rows and long, straight paths that the people of that time loved processionals. Imagine a scene from the past: the priests in front are walking grandly, possibly with deer skull headdresses, painted bodies, and accompanied by the sounds of bone flutes and drums. Behind them the sacrificial animals are being led, covered in flowers and herbs. A large number of young maidens and men walk behind, circling around each of the stones, followed by the rest of the tribe.

Most ritual landscapes featured causewayed enclosures, which were in fact some of the first constructions. Windmill Hill is probably the earliest causewayed camp in Britain. Often sited in the same area as the original settlement, these large land areas were composed of ditches and banks, and were usually located on hills. They are distinct from the later hillforts because of their two or more entrances, or causeways, that render the centre vulnerable. These areas were set aside for ritual slaughter and feasting, and judging from the amount of foreign pottery and axes, were also used for trading. Most have produced great quantities of animal and human bones in the ditches, which may to us seem like a rather irreverent way to treat the dead.

Windmill Hill

Below:
Part of the West Kennet Avenue. The Beckhampton Avenue is mostly obliterated.

West Kennet Long Barrow

Below:

The Sanctuary is one of the oldest sites in the Avebury complex. This funerary house was originally made of timber and possibly thatch, and a scale model of it can be viewed at the Devizes Museum.

The West Kennet Long Barrow is one of the biggest and oldest of all the barrows in Britain. Situated on top of a hill close to Avebury and next to Silbury, it was constructed of local sarsens topped with chalk, so that the whole monument would have stood out gleaming white. Later, a forecourt was added, probably to provide a place for funerary rites. Inside the tomb a straight passage ended with a burial chamber. Branching off from the main passage are four side chambers, used to roughly divide the sexes and ages. These compartments were capped by huge sarsen slabs. Over a period of a thousand years or more, forty-six people were buried inside. Many of the dead were children, who usually didn't have enough status for that kind of attention. The heads and longbones of at least some of the corpses had been taken away to use in ceremonies elsewhere.

The final interment was of an old man during the Beaker phase. He had an arrowpoint in his neck, undoubtedly the cause of death. After the barrow ceased to be in use, it was purposely filled with rubble (probably sacred earth from other ceremonial sites), and sealed with the huge sarsens that blocked the original crescent-shaped courtyard.

The children could have died from any of the common causes – flu, measles or pneumonia (since these don't leave scars on bone, we'll never know). Examination of the rest of the skeletons showed that nearly all the adults had spinal arthritis from living in cold, damp conditions. Some had twisted arms and legs, and the males had bone fractures probably received from fights. The teeth had abscesses and impacted wisdom teeth, although there were very few cavities. Some of the people even lived to the ripe old age

Left & right:
The interior and exterior of West Kennet Long Barrow.

of thirty-five! A Dr Toope of Marlborough came in 1685 and stole many of the bones 'of which I made a noble medicine that relieved my distressed neighbours'.

Silbury Hill was the largest man-made hill in all of pre-historic Europe, and also the most labour-intensive piece of construction in Neolithic Britain; it would have taken 800 men ten years to build, if they worked all year round. It was begun about the same time as the pyramids, around 2700 BC. From a base of $5\frac{1}{4}$ acres, the hill rises to 130 feet (40 metres), and contains $12\frac{1}{2}$ million cubic feet of chalk and soil. The ditch around it was originally 16 feet (nearly 5 metres) deep and 70 feet (over 20 metres) wide.

It wasn't always that grandiose. Its first phase was originally just a circle 120 feet (36 metres) in diameter, next to the very sacred River Kennet. Gravel from the riverbed and chalk turves were heaped on top of the circle, followed by layers of soil, clay, chalk and gravel from the riverbed, until it rose to 15 feet (4.5 metres) in height. In the second phase, an area double the size of the first was laid out, with a ditch excavated next to it. This monument was built out of chalk blocks quarried from the hillside. These were then formed into sloping steps, and held together by wattle walls. It was about 55 feet (nearly 17 metres) high, but was only partially finished when it was superseded by an even grander design.

Silbury Hill

Phase I

Phase II

Below:
Another one of Stukeley's many drawings of the Avebury complex.

Prospect of the Temple on Overton Hill. 8 July 1723.

TAB XXI
P.40.

The Hakpen, or head of the Snake, in ruins.

Phase III

Silbury Hill is the largest man-made mound in Europe.

The third phase completely covered over everything that went before; the earlier ditch was filled in and replaced by an even larger one. The new mound was a bigger replica of the earlier one, with the same slope of 30 degrees. It was made from six concentric steps, each about 15 feet high, built one on top of the other, like a giant layer cake. Each tier was made of chalk cells that were infilled with a mixture of chalk, rubble and silt. The entire project would have required three million man-hours to complete so it must have been an important place.

A monument this big was bound to attract attention. Although it was ignored by the Bronze Age and Iron Age people, King

Charles II found it interesting enough to walk to the top with Aubrey, who wrote that the local people believed 'that the hill was raysed while a posset of milk was seething.' It was also thought to be the resting place of a King Sel who was buried astride his horse, all in gold. On certain nights, it was said that you could see him riding around the base of the hill. All this talk of gold had the usual effect, and no less than four separate excavations were attempted, between 1776 and 1968. Although the first dig did find moss that was still practically green, some ox bones and a deer tooth, no one was ever to find a single thing of monetary value.

However, Silbury Hill may have been a massive fertility figure, the pregnant womb of the Mother Goddess, so universal to primitive farming societies. During the mid-to-late Neolithic, the soil had been depleted through over-use, and the population had increased dramatically. We can assume that the Kennet, and especially Swallowhead Spring, the mouth of the Kennet, had close associations with the female deity. With the quarry dug close to the water table, perhaps Silbury was a giant monument to the Goddess, surrounded by her holy waters, a desperate plea to her to bring fertility to the land. In particular, the goddess Sul was very important throughout much of the south-western area of England in those times. She was certainly important enough that the Romans adopted her when they named their great baths Aquae Sulis. And even more importantly, her worship was noted by historians to take place on the tops of hills, close to holy streams!

Since nothing was found inside it (and the same is true of the mounds at Marlborough and Marden in Wiltshire and Knowlton in Dorset), the mound itself must have been what was important.

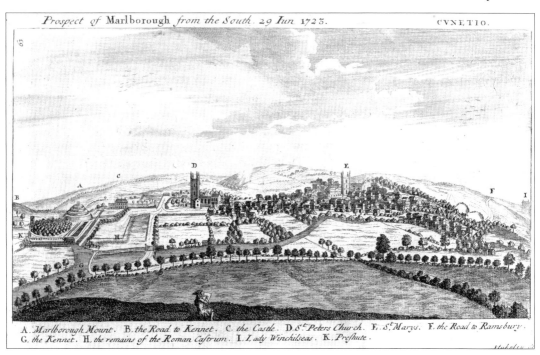

Prospect of Marlborough *from the South. 29 Iun 1723.*　　　　　CVNETIO.

A. *Marlborough Mount*. B. *the Road to Kennet*. C. *the Castle*. D. *St Peters Church*. E. *St Marys*. F. *the Road to Ramsbury*. G. *the Kennet*. H. *the remains of the Roman Castrum*. I. *Lady Winchilseas*. K. *Preshute*.

Left:
It is hard for us to imagine the tremendous amount of effort it would have taken Neolithic Man, using only antler picks and ox shoulderblade shovels, to erect this massive monument.

However, sited as it is in a river valley, it is not suited as a beacon or proud display of territory. It may be a monument to commemorate a famous battle, or a fallen chieftain.

No matter what it was erected for, it would have taken an enormous amount of organisation of resources from a highly respected supreme ruler or ruling class. Built during the middle Neolithic, a time of great social change and uncertainty, perhaps the building was the point.

Far left:
This sketch of Marlborough by John Aubrey clearly shows its mound, supposedly the resting place of Merlin. This is how the town allegedly got its name.

As a part of the fertility aspect, the hill could also have been used yearly as a massive Harvest Hill. And Silbury wouldn't have been an isolated one, because certain hills were used throughout Britain for Harvest festivals, and where there weren't any suitable hills, the populations would erect their own. In a continuation of the fertility theme, folklore suggests that a Harvest Queen or maiden would sit at the top of the hill, bedecked with garlands of flowers. Other girls would dance around her, picking off the flowers in a frenzied celebration.

Old religions die hard, and as late as the eighteenth century, Stukeley noted that 'the country people have an anniversary meeting on top of Silbury-hill, on every Palm Sunday, where they make merry with cakes, figs, sugar, and water fetched from the swallow head, or spring of the Kennet.'

SOUTH WALES

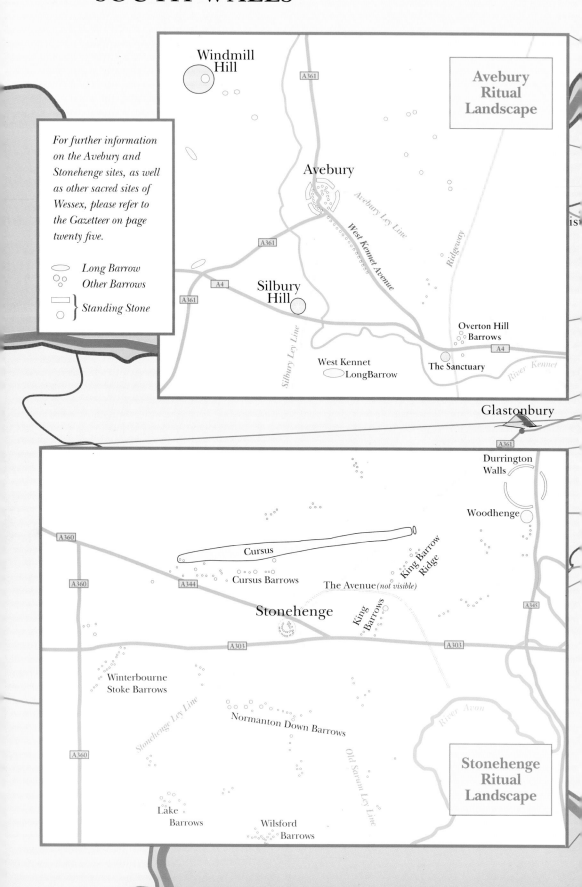

Avebury Ritual Landscape

Windmill Hill

A361

Avebury

Avebury Ley Line

Ridgeway

West Kennet Avenue

A361

A361

A4

Silbury Hill

Silbury Ley Line

Overton Hill Barrows

A4

West Kennet LongBarrow

The Sanctuary

River Kennet

For further information on the Avebury and Stonehenge sites, as well as other sacred sites of Wessex, please refer to the Gazetteer on page twenty five.

Long Barrow
Other Barrows
} Standing Stone

Glastonbury

A361

Durrington Walls

Woodhenge

A360

Cursus

King Barrow Ridge

A360

A344

Cursus Barrows

The Avenue (not visible)

A345

Stonehenge

King Barrows

A303

A303

Winterbourne Stoke Barrows

Stonehenge Ley Line

Normanton Down Barrows

River Avon

Old Sarum Ley Line

A360

Stonehenge Ritual Landscape

Lake Barrows

Wilsford Barrows

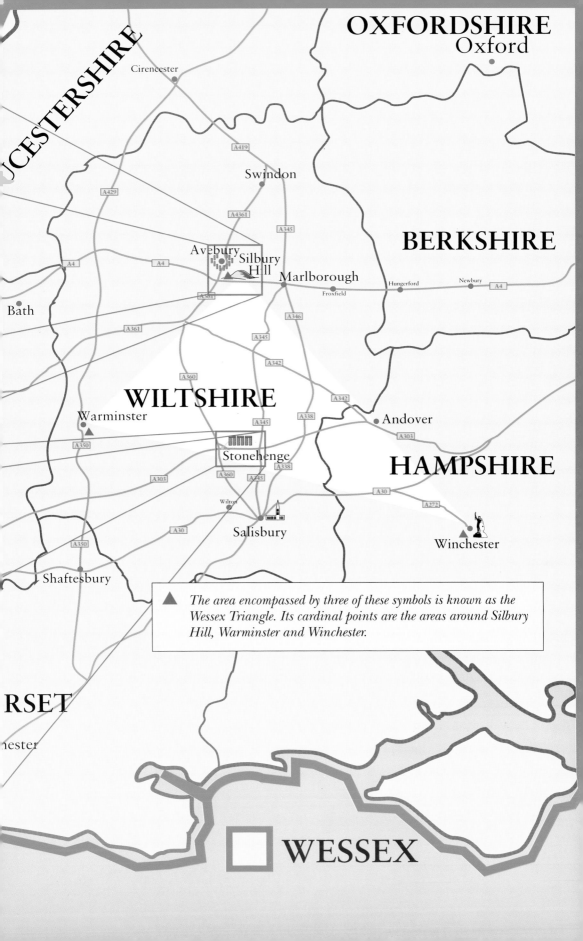

OXFORDSHIRE
Oxford

BERKSHIRE

—CESTERSHIRE

Cirencester

A419

A429

Swindon

A4361

A345

Avebury Silbury
Hill

Marlborough

Hungerford

Newbury
A4

Froxfield

A4

A4

Bath

A361

A361

A345

A346

A360

A345

A342

WILTSHIRE

A342

Warminster

A345

A338

Andover

A350

A303

Stonehenge

A338

HAMPSHIRE

A303

A360

A345

A30

A272

Wilton

Winchester

A30

Salisbury

A350

Shaftesbury

▲ *The area encompassed by three of these symbols is known as the Wessex Triangle. Its cardinal points are the areas around Silbury Hill, Warminster and Winchester.*

—RSET

—hester

☐ WESSEX

The Stonehenge Complex

In common with Avebury and the Dorset Ridgeway, THE STONEHENGE COMPLEX is dominated by a density of Neolithic and Bronze Age monuments. Stonehenge lies on Salisbury Plain about 13km north of Salisbury and about the same south of Avebury. To look at the area today, you may wonder why anyone would want to live here. However, since the climate was warmer thousands of years ago, the soil was in better shape and because the area was surrounded by forest – it was a perfect spot for Neolithic farmers. As in other ritual landscapes, the area around Stonehenge itself was not inhabited, perhaps because of a taboo.

The henge in history

Above:

Stonehenge drawn soon after a 1920s excavation.

Stonehenge is one of the most famous sites in the world; the henge was well known even in Roman times, and was first described in writing in 1130 AD. Speculation throughout the centuries about its origins have been many and varied. Perhaps it was raised by Merlin at the request of King Arthur, or by Mycenaeans, whose architecture it resembled. Perhaps it was Roman, or Danish. But by 1697, when John Aubrey died, it was finally accepted that Stonehenge was made by British ancestors. Later, William Stukeley visited the site in 1719, returning every year to map and draw the area. He discovered the Avenue leading into the circle, and traced it as far as King Barrow Ridge (it actually travels all the

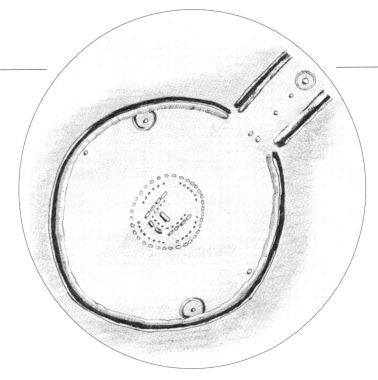

Left:
A floorplan of Stonehenge phase III, when the site was at its apex. This configuration of stones, it has been argued, is typical of French (Breton) rather than English (British) neolithic constructions. Perhaps it was our earliest import from across the channel. It will, no doubt, provide food for much archaeological argument in the years to come.

way to the river Avon). Later he found the Cursus, another enigmatic earthwork to be found near many Neolithic henges. After digging in the numerous barrows, Stukeley proclaimed that they were the 'sepulchres of kings, and great personages, buried during a considerable space of time'. And as at Avebury, he stuck by his theory that the site was built and used by Druids, a completely erroneous idea that is still believed today.

What did Stonehenge look like originally? To begin with, it was built and re-built over a period of about 1800 years. We can only see the huge stones now, but judging from other circles it was probably made out of wood to begin with, and most likely had a circular wooden building in the centre.

The first phase of the structure began around 2800 BC. Then, it was just a henge, with a bank and ditch. The ditch was found to be irregular in depth, varying from four to seven feet, with the bank being about six feet. This proves the notion that ditches were dug in different sections by different groups, some obviously more robust than others. The Heel Stone, the only stone outside the circle, was erected along with its now lost twin. There were also four station stones, of which two remain. Finally, a ring of 56 pits known as Aubrey Holes were left inside the bank. They were dug, and then immediately filled again, sometimes with cremated remains. They may have been used to count the cycles of the moon, or to predict eclipses. However, the latter suggestion would require a very advanced knowledge of the lunar orbit.

The original Stonehenge

Stonehenge,
J.M.W. Turner.

A prominent Avenue led to the henge, which must originally have been intended as a basic lunar observatory. Since the moon has a complicated cycle of nearly nineteen years, the priests must have been watching the skies for a long time. The area was re-aligned 800 years later along the midsummer sunrise/midwinter sunset axis.

What is Stonehenge? It is the roofless past,
Man's ruinous myth, his uninterred adoring of the unknown.
Sunrise cold and red,
His quest of stars that arch his doomed exploring.
And what is time, but shadows that were cast by these
Storm sculptured stones while centuries fled?
The stones remain.
Their stillness can outlast the skies of history
Hurrying overhead.

WILLIAM BLAKE

Built along with the first phase of Stonehenge was the Cursus, **The Cursus**
an area about 330 feet wide and over two miles long close to the
henge. The banks at the ends were higher than the sides, which
lead Stukeley (who discovered it) to assume he had found a
Roman hippodrome for chariot racing – he even drew the ends
rounded, when in fact they were squared off. Although the area
has been excavated and examined, nobody knows what function it
had really. It seems very likely (from the number of stone corridors
erected), that the Neolithic people loved processions, so perhaps it
was a sort of red carpet in which processions, ritual races and
sporting games were held.

The second Stonehenge – bluestones

About 700 years later, the area was revived with the addition of the bluestones. The name bluestone is misleading, because they aren't one single type of rock, they're just from one place – the Preseli Mountains in south-west Wales. One of the types of rock, rhyolite, does take on a blue-grey colour when wet. The bluestones (82 in all) were ferried around the coast of South Wales and into the Avon at Bristol, down that and the Frome, then overland six miles to the River Wylye at Warminster, along the river until it joined the Avon at Salisbury, and finally two miles overland to Stonehenge. Why go to all that trouble?

The bluestones were set up in two concentric circles, with the Altar Stone in the centre. About 16 feet long, this is also foreign to the area, made of micaceous sandstone and scattered with very fine pieces of garnet. It was probably picked up on the bluestone route. It now lies flat and mostly buried, but originally stood upright, and so was unlikely to have been used for sacrifices. This stone arrangement seemed satisfactory for about a hundred years.

The third Stonehenge – sarsens

Around 2000 BC, the bluestone circle was dismantled, leaving the stones lying around the immediate area. Sarsen stones must have been brought from the Marlborough Downs 18 miles away, carried on sledges with wooden rollers, pulled with cords made from sinew or plant fibres, by a combination of men and animals.

The 77 sarsens, each weighing many tonnes, were moved one by one to the edge of a ramp, then tipped into a hole at the bottom and finally, somehow, tilted upright, and the hole filled with chalk

Above:
Stone'enge,
Thomas Rowlandson,
circa 1784.

and earth. Then more refinements were made, creating the curvature at the top of the massive trilithons (literally 'three stone'), and also creating the illusion of height by deliberately making the tops narrower than the bases. Again, somehow, the lintels were raised into place on top, their mortises fitting neatly into the tenons already in place. Maybe a wooden crib was built that the lintel rested on, and slowly increased in height until it reached the top of the upright. Or perhaps a huge bank of earth was built that created a slope in which to pull the upright into position.

The Great Trilithon, five groups of the largest stones, were set in a horseshoe with the open end facing the axis. The Sarsen Circle, with a diameter of nearly 100 feet, was made of thirty stones, each with a lintel; 17 of the uprights, and five of the lintels, still stand, their average weight about 26 tonnes. The Slaughter Stone, so called because of its reddish colour (actually the result of rain reacting with the iron in it), was erected at this time. Also, a number of the round barrows in the area were erected.

A little further on in time, someone must have noticed the bluestones lying around, wasted, and so erected them in an oval shape within the Trilithons. This was not to last long, and about 1550 BC the bluestones were dismantled again and re-erected as a bluestone ring that also opened on the axis. This was the final stage of construction, before the area was presumably taken over by a different culture with a different set of beliefs. But the site had been used for over 1500 years.

> **The healing stones:**
> *It has been suggested*
> *that the bluestones were*
> *already part of an*
> *existing stone circle in*
> *Wales before being*
> *uprooted and taken to*
> *Salisbury Plain. That*
> *circle would have been*
> *well known, perhaps for*
> *healing powers. On the*
> *subject of Stonehenge,*
> *Geoffrey of Monmouth*
> *wrote that* 'there is
> not a stone there
> which has not some
> healing virtue'.

The purpose of Stonehenge

It has been calculated that it would have taken over 3000 man-years to prepare and transport the sarsens (and quite a few acres of woodland). That translates into five hundred men working all year for three-and-a-half years.

What was it used for? Probably, like Avebury, it was used to mark important dates in the calendar, especially midsummer and midwinter. Ceremonies that dealt with marriages, death, fertility and harvest were probably practised. There is a strong emphasis on water, so perhaps a water goddess was worshipped, such as Sul. Judging from other cultures and folklore, there would have been

much dancing and wild merry making, along with constant music from chanting, drums and flutes.

Although in the surrounding area there were a great number of burials, there were only a very few associated with Stonehenge itself. One is that of The Archer, a Beaker period man who was found buried with his stone wrist guard, and who also had arrowheads imbedded in him, which must have caused his death.

Stonehenge, like Avebury, is part of a larger ritual complex. The area is littered with other sites of ritual use, some of which are located on the map on page 14 and listed on page 25.

The Heel Stone, an outlying rock not visible in this picture, is so called because legend states that the Devil threw the stone at a monk, striking his heel and leaving a mark on the stone, which is still visible today.

Neolithic people – a farming community

When the first farming people arose out of the earlier Mesolithic hunter-gatherer tribes in Britain, much of the upper Wessex area, especially in Wiltshire, was carpeted in a thick forest, which was soon cleared, most likely using the slash-and-burn method. Once the land was cleared, the area was used heavily for agricultural purposes, which eventually led to the soil's depletion.

These Neolithic people looked physically similar to us, wore clothes made not only from animal skins, but also linen and wool. The clothes might have been embroidered, or had designs painted on them. Judging from other primitive groups, we can assume that the people were tattooed, and possibly wore elaborate hairstyles. They grew six-rowed and naked barley (the most common), and also emmer, bread and einkorn wheats, flax and spelt. They made use of what the environment around them had to offer, such as hazelnuts and crabapples, fish, snails, a number of small birds, deer and boar. The settlements were probably thatched huts near the streams and rivers, with animal pens for the sheep, goats, cattle and pigs, alongside the small granaries and pits.

Long barrows

Since land rights were so important, the farming community was probably organised into several family groups, with ties to each other through a remote ancestor (buried in the long barrow). These farmers developed the long barrow in which to bury their dead, mainly because they weren't that hard to build, and the early pastoral communities probably couldn't afford the time and energy to make anything more ostentatious. But even these long barrows used precious resources, so why build them in the first place?

In most primitive farming societies, land is owned because of family rights, starting with original real or imagined ancestor's claims. In this way, long barrows laid claim to the land and were therefore a very good investment as they honoured the ancestors, and served as territorial markers. The first stages of some of the causewayed camps and henges were constructed, too, probably as a means of increasing the tribe's sense of togetherness. Since the climate was warmer and wetter than it is now, there was abundant game and arable land. Life was good.

Causewayed camps

Prehistoric recession

But nothing good lasts forever, and within a few hundred years, the area became over populated, the soil depleted and there was fighting and killing taking place amongst a previously peaceful population. There was no time for building monuments.

Gazetteer

✛ *Adam's Grave Long Barrow*
Amesbury Down Triple Bell Barrow
✛ *Avebury*
Bush Barrow
> The Bush Barrow is one of the most important barrows ever excavated.

Clatford Circle
Clifford's Hill Causewayed Camp
Coneybury Henge
Cursus Barrows
Danebury Long Barrows
✛ *Devil's Den Barrow*
> Supposedly haunted by a phantom dog.

Durrington Walls
> A huge henge, about 1500 feet in diameter. In past times the site of feasting and conspicuous consumption on a grand scale. Best viewed from Woodhenge.

East Kennet Long Barrow
Enford Bowl Barrow
Fargo Wood
✛ *Gatcombe Lodge Chambered Cairn*
✛ *Giant's Cave Long Cairn*
✛ *Giant's Grave Long Barrow*
Gopher Wood Barrow Cemetery
Grafton Disc Barrows
✛ *Hetty Pegler's Tump Long Cairn*
> Best preserved cairn in the Costswolds.

Horslip Long Barrow
Inkpen Long Barrow
✛ *King Barrows*
✛ *Knap Hill Causewayed Camp*
✛ *Lake Downs Barrows*
Lamborough Banks Chambered Cairn
Lambourn Seven Barrows
Manton Down Long Barrow
✛ *Marden Henge*
> A large henge now barely visible.

✛ *Marlborough Mound*
> Similar to Silbury and said to be the resting place of Merlin.

Millbarrow Long Barrow
Nan Tow's Tump
✛ *Normanton Down Barrows*

✛ *Overton Hill Barrows*
> Directly opposite the Sanctuary.

Robin Hood's Ball
✛ *Rollright Stones*
> The most important stone circle in Oxfordshire.

Roughridge Hill Long Barrow
✛ *The Sanctuary*
Shelving Stones Barrow
✛ *Silbury Hill*
Snail Down Barrow Cemetery
South Street Long Barrow
✛ *Stanton Drew*
> Important stone circle south of Bristol.

✛ *The Stonehenge Cursus*
Temple Bottom Long Barrow
✛ *Tingle Stone Long Cairn*
> Holed standing stone through which babies were passed to ensure good health.

✛ *Wayland's Smithy*
> Well preseved chamber tomb near the Uffington White Horse

✛ *West Kennet Long Barrow*
West Woods Long Barrow
White Sheet Hill Causewayed Camp
Wilsford Downs Barrows
Wilsford Down North Kite
✛ *Windmill Hill*
✛ *Winterbourne Stoke Group (barrows)*
> Many different types of barrows can be found on this one site near Stonehenge.

✛ *Woodhenge*
> A circular structure, possibly a funerary house. Near the centre was a grave containing the skeleton of a child about three years old, whose skull was split either accidentally or as a sacrifice.

The sites marked with ✛ are easily visited. Please refer to the map on page 14 for general location. Other sites, although important, are either inaccessible or badly damaged.

Beaker people

Above:
Neolithic Man.

All of the sites had reverted to scrubland through neglect. In other words, they were in the middle of a recession. In some cases, people who used to be cereal growers reverted to hunting game. It was about this time that the Beaker people came to power. These short, swarthy folk set about rebuilding the monuments, making them even greater. Although costly in terms of resources, it would have been a deliberate strategy for maintaining power and control when the fabric of society had decayed. The actual process of building would have focused society at large and helped to promote a group image.

Pigs started to replace other farm animals, because they were ideally suited for the times. Their rooting nature would aerate the soil, and they fed on the bracken that had taken over. In addition, their quick reproduction rate and large litters provided the nourishment for a population that had a lot of extra mouths to feed while the building phase was going on. The red deer that roamed the forests were also used wisely. Instead of killing the deer, the

Beaker people managed their populations so that there were always lots of cast off antlers to use for construction purposes within walking distance of the henges.

The sites could have been places of status for powerful people, or centres for the learned elite, like the magician/astronomers, who would have studied full time while the population supported them. Or they could be likened to modern cathedrals. They certainly were embedded with a sense of power, and not just of the religious kind.

It is reasonable to suppose that the people thousands of years ago could feel the subtle earth energy forces that run through the earth. The circles themselves might have acted as power accelerators, with the magnetic and electric properties of some of the rocks being released by dancing, or through the careful siting of the monument on a ley. The priests, already attuned to the special frequencies of the stones, could then harness their power to enable them to better heal people and predict the future.

Construction of henges

Above:
Early Bronze Age/Beaker Man.

Afterthought

We know what our ancestors' tools and ritual objects look like. We even know what they ate, how they buried their dead, the natural surroundings of their world. But there will always be many things we don't know.

Why do we feel a need to look back, thousands of years through the mists of time? Are we searching for something precious that we've lost? In our modern world, these ancient landscapes are fleetingly glimpsed as we hurtle down the motorway. Our feet rarely touch the earth; when we look skyward, we see the ceiling in our dining room. Even our places of worship are sealed off from the outdoors. Is it any wonder that we can no longer feel the same lines of energy running underfoot, that our ancestors undoubtedly felt?

We look back in an attempt to capture that feeling of oneness with the earth, where the rocks, pools, hills and valleys are vibrantly alive. We look back to a time of mysteries and wonders, where invocations and ceremonies were an indispensable part of everyday life in a direct link to the divine.

If we take the time to slow down and listen, these prehistoric tombs and temples may speak to us yet.

Right:
The floor plan of Avebury as it would have appeared over 4000 years ago.

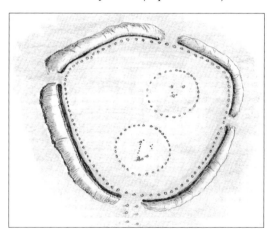

Brief Bibliography

Michael Dames, *The Avebury Cycle*, Thames and Hudson, 1977
Caroline Malone, *English Heritage Book of Avebury*, B.T. Batsford Ltd. London '89
Julian Richards, *English Heritage Book of Stonehenge*, B.T. Batsford, London 1991
George Terence Meaden, *The Goddess of the Stones*, Souvenir Press, London, 1991
Geoffrey Wainwright, *The Henge Monuments*, Thames and Hudson, London 1989
Aubrey Burl, *Rings of Stone*, Frances Lincoln Ltd. London, 1979
Michael Dames, *The Silbury Treasure*, Thames and Hudson, London, 1976
Michael Balfour, *Stonehenge and Its Mysteries*, McDonald & Janes, London, 1979

4500 BC	*Late Mesolithic*	Hunter-gatherers, woodlands.	*Round-bottomed pottery and arrowheads. Long barrows*
4200 BC	*Early Neolithic*	Clearance of forest. First barrows.	*and causewayed camps built.*
3700 BC	"	Settlement on Windmill Hill. Focus on Avebury area. West Kennet Long Barrow erected. More fields and settlements.	*Early farming communities, with an emphasis on group burial (known as Windmill*
3500 BC	"	Causewayed camps built. Robin Hood's Ball camp. First Stonehenge.	*Hill Culture).*
3000 BC	*Middle Neo.*	Phase I of Sanctuary started. Flint tools.	*Henge monuments began to*
2700 BC	"	Phase II of Sanctuary. Phase I of Silbury Hill.	*be erected.*
2600 BC	*Late Neolithic*	Avebury begun.	*Rise of the people of the*
2500 BC	"	Phase II Silbury Hill; Phase III Sanctuary. Marden, Woodhenge and Durrington Walls henges built.	*Wessex Culture, who constructed the numerous round barrows*
2400 BC	"	Avebury stones. Avenues erected. Long barrows not in use.	*that speckle the landscape. This society developed a hierarchy,*
2200 BC	"	Ceremonial landscapes.	*at the top of which were powerful chieftains, who were*
2000 BC	*Bronze Age*	Second Stonehenge – bluestones. Sarsen circle erected later.	*buried along with grave goods that included gold, amber,*
1900 BC	"	Avebury in decline. Round barrows. Wessex culture.	*glass, bronze daggers, beads*
1800 BC	"	Third Stonehenge.	*and jewellery.*

WESSEX BOOKS

Watch out for other titles in
THE WESSEX SERIES
- Vineyards of Wessex
- Thomas Hardy of Wessex
- Wessex Goes to the Movies
- King Arthur in Wessex
- Women of Wessex • Haunted Wessex
- The Story of Wessex
- Jane Austen in Wessex
- Great Religious Houses of Wessex
- Travellers in Wessex
from:
Wessex Books, 2 Station Cottages,
Newton Toney, Salisbury,
Wiltshire SP4 0HD

Acknowledgements

For the use of illustrations and photographs not supplied by the author, the publishers gratefully thank:

Jürgen Krönig, pp. 3,6,7,10,26;
Salisbury and South Wiltshire Museum, pp.16,18,20;
Kim Williams Photography, front cover, pp. 2,22;
Wiltshire Archaeological & Natural History Society, pp. 5,9,12.

Cover illustration by Andrew Stewart Jamieson. Cover panel and centre map, design and computer typesetting produced by Alexander S. Grenfell. Edited by Jane Drake.

Published by Wessex Books 1997.
Text © Kent Goodman.

This book is dedicated to Terrie, Tom and Noah.

Printed in Great Britain by B.A.S. Printers.

ISBN 0 9529619 1 1

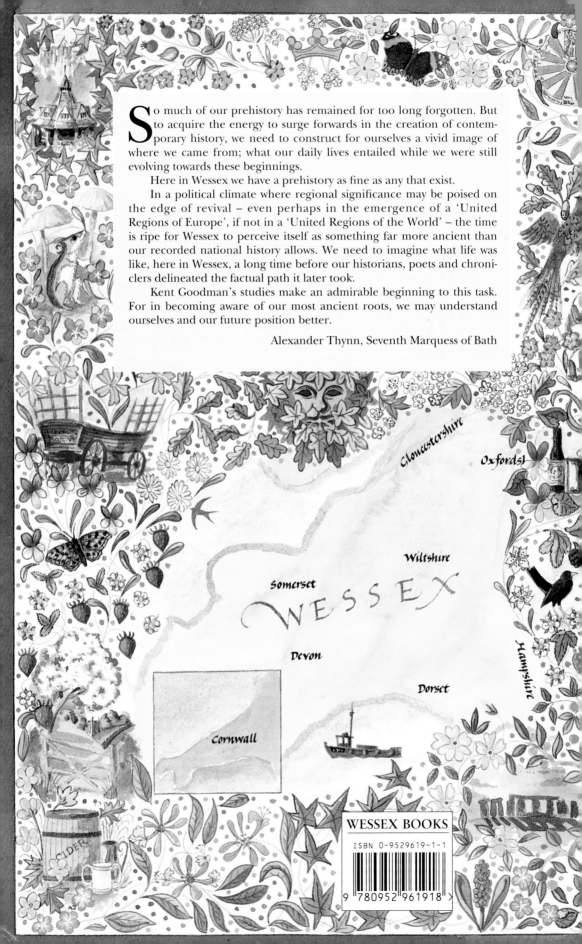

So much of our prehistory has remained for too long forgotten. But to acquire the energy to surge forwards in the creation of contemporary history, we need to construct for ourselves a vivid image of where we came from; what our daily lives entailed while we were still evolving towards these beginnings.

Here in Wessex we have a prehistory as fine as any that exist.

In a political climate where regional significance may be poised on the edge of revival – even perhaps in the emergence of a 'United Regions of Europe', if not in a 'United Regions of the World' – the time is ripe for Wessex to perceive itself as something far more ancient than our recorded national history allows. We need to imagine what life was like, here in Wessex, a long time before our historians, poets and chroniclers delineated the factual path it later took.

Kent Goodman's studies make an admirable beginning to this task. For in becoming aware of our most ancient roots, we may understand ourselves and our future position better.

Alexander Thynn, Seventh Marquess of Bath

Gloucestershire

Oxfords[

Wiltshire

Somerset

WESSEX

Devon

Hampshire

Dorset

Cornwall

WESSEX BOOKS

ISBN 0-9529619-1-1

9 780952 961918